Angel Pages

By Kimberly Ann Borin

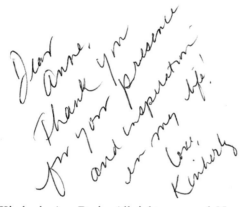

All illustrations in *Angel Pages* by Kimberly Ann Borin, ©2015
Angel Pages front and back cover design by Kimberly Borin, ©2015
Formatting by: Judy Loose, www.looselinks.com
Digital coloring of illustrations in images in *Grace to Go* chapter
by Natalie Crum of Digital Arts Imaging.

ISBN-13: 978-1503253001 (CreateSpace-Assigned)
ISBN-10: 1503253007
LCCN: 2015900303

Dedication

This book is dedicated to my mom.
She is an Angel who inspires everyone
with her love, strength, beauty, and creativity.

Table of Contents

Introduction

Angel Pages

Angel Pages are playful drawings filled to the brim with inspiration, love, and encouragement. This book is a collection of the designs with caring words, whimsical art, and heartfelt prayers. I offer these to you with the hope that they will nourish your heart and spirit. I hope that the tender voice within the art gives you the courage, peace, and strength you need to live into your dreams.

In the art you will see that you are a gift, you have a gift, and you get to choose how to move forward on your journey. In the pages, you will be offered gentle permission and the chance to believe in your most beautiful hopes. Most importantly, the pages will remind you that ***you are deeply loved***.

I started creating *Angel Pages* in 2001. When I sat down with my morning cup of coffee, I also sat with a white pad of paper, and a fine line marker. This is one way that I began to pray and how I created *Angel Pages*. Now, when I sit down to write, I trust that the words and designs will come, and they will stop when it is time. I trust that I will also receive a comforting answer and inspiration. When I sit, I often create seven or eight pieces with a particular theme and never do any of them twice. When I write, I see my worries, prayers, and hopes spill onto the page. I also see a response and answer that is loving, encouraging, and positive.

I am always surprised at what ends up on the paper and I always feel peaceful and comforted in reading what I have written. Sometimes weeks, months, or years later, I am still surprised at what I have written, and how much I still need the words. I am often in awe of how the words have comforted others as well, sometimes offering just the answer they needed. I hope that these *Angel Pages* will offer you the peace and encouragement you need to breathe life into your dreams.

Ideas for Using *Angel Pages*

Below are some simple ways to use this book. Of course, you will come up with your own ways – and they will be *just right*. Here are some other ideas for using the words or art for inspiration.

In this book you can focus on the words within each piece of art. You may want to take a moment to be with the art and notice what word or words capture your attention. You may want to pray or meditate about those words – or even begin to journal and see what is revealed to you. There are 75 pieces of art that offer words of comfort, compassion, hope, and more. See which words you need for today!

In this book you can also focus on the art, the color, or the movement of the piece. You may want to notice what piece of art resonates with you and then explore what it means for your journey. I have divided the art up into three categories: *Designs in Play*, *Grace to Go*, and *Healing Words for the Journey*. They have been created at different times in my life but I have placed them together because they have similar patterns and colors.

The Journal Pages

At the end of the book you will find several blank journal pages with some encouraging words. You may want to use this space for journaling, drawing, writing stories, or even your favorite recipe. The intention of the pages is for you to have space to create and be encouraged. You may also want to check out the companion journal, *Angel Pages for You*, for more journaling inspiration.

Blessings for You

I hope that this little book of art offers you peace for your journey and nourishment for your spirit and heart. I hope that the *Angel Pages* will remind you of how precious you are and that you are deeply loved. I am wishing you many blessings of peace, creativity, and love on your journey

Designs

In

Play

Take a chance

Tell Your STORY

Once time... In a la away... And on't moon... With a I dance Singing out loud I journeyed to my

Follow Your ♥

whisper.
Choose
LOVE
Be present.
seek grace

Have Mighty Faith

Take Your Time.

Dream BOLDLY!

Listen for Angels.

Trust what you feel.

Believe in Your dreams.
Yes! Yes! Yes!

6

7

8

You Are Blessed!!

Have Faith.

Be Brave!

You and The Angels will breathe life into your most beautiful dreams your most sacred journey.

Kimberly 12/02

Gather Support!

Take Action.

Believe!

10

I want you to know and BELIEVE that You are Precious! To the World and Life itself loved... You are...

Oh to steal away. to Dream. Imagine. Write. Read. Color and D.R.A.W.! And maybe just have quiet moments of tea and reflection.

Kimberly Brown 2/01

Beautiful Child of God, It is your time to Blossom!

ANGELS

Today,
I will call to things unseen.
I will ask for miracles,
I will whisper for angels,
I will pray for deeper faith.
I will speak about trust and believing,
I will reach and dream about my journey
I will call to things unseen.

11/01 Kimberly Brink

BELIEVE

Today,
May life reach
out to you.
Allow her to call to
you, embrace you.
Sing to you.
May she heal and
uphold you and
bear your beautiful
D r e a m s.
May she deliver you
in mercy and
grace.

1/01
Kimberly

May ☆
the
child in you
sing, 🤍
believe,
hope, be,
play. 🌀
rejoice
☆ and rest.
If even for a
🤍 moment
today.
Joy to you!

Kimberly
Brown

16

18

Believe in your dreams and dream big!

Grace

Peace

You are a gift to the World!

celebrate!

Hope and Trust

You are an amazing Creation of love, beauty, magic and miracles You are deeply loved.

Kymberly Morin 12/01

20

The Recipe...

1 morning of...
Thankfulness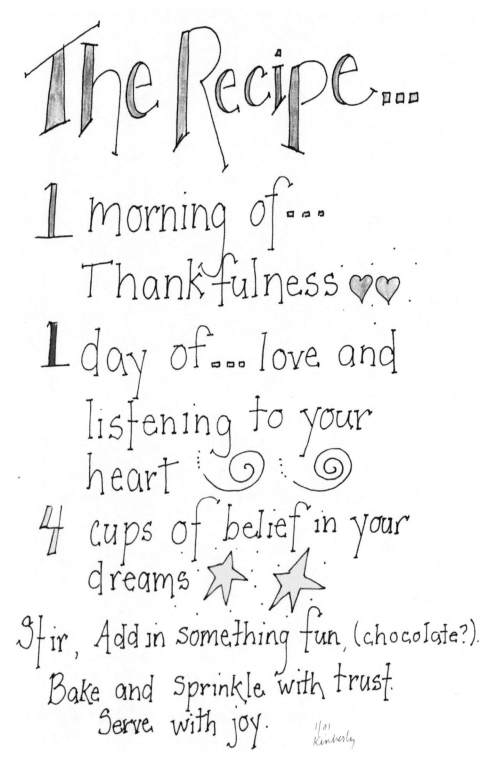
1 day of... love and
listening to your
heart
4 cups of belief in your
dreams

Stir, Add in something fun, (chocolate?).
Bake and sprinkle with trust.
Serve with joy.

1/01
Kimberly

22

Some
Comfort
to
ponder...
pastel
quilts,
the beach,
love,
hope and stars
for wishes.

23

24

I will
Create anew
with water.
Sunlight fresh air,
prayer and color.
I will invite friends
and family to create
with me. I will draw,
paint, breathe, walk, sing
and dream. I know that
moment by moment my
transformation will unfold in
the most beautiful way.

Love,
Me.

1/2/01
Kimberley

In time, you will know what must be. In time your heart and hands and spirit will be ready. In time, it will be clear and effortless to decide. You will know....

1/01
Kimberly

Dance, Dare, Dream and then Some....

WOW

28

29

Just as the plant waits to BLOOM you are waiting too. Child your time is coming to Blossom in ways that will stretch what you know about Beauty.

Grace

Beauty

Hope

Love

Kimberly Brown

Grace

To

Go

33

Angels ♥

A special invitation just for angels of mercy, grace and love.

Have an angel moment party!

Celebrate Angels and Invites

Please visit today ... ♡

...to offer hope and tenderness,
to hold a hand,
to wipe a tear.
R. S. V. P. at any old time.
Thank you for the gift you are!

11/01 Kimberly Bain

34

35

36

39

Decorate

Breathe in Blessings, Decorate with Peace, Plant seeds of Miracles... Be the gardener of GRACE.

Kimberly Bonn 5/8 11/14

40

Be held by Grace

Have Hope

Trust in what you see.

Some Light for Today...

Listen

offer Yourself every Kindness

Take small steps.

Magic

Nourish your Beautiful Self

Be Brave.

Possibility

Dream in Color!

Take a gentle chance

Miracle Stories

Follow Your ♥

Believe, Child.

12/2013 Kimberly Brown

TRUST-

Take all of the Time that you need to decide, to move, to speak, to choose. You will know what to do when the time is right. TRUST.

Please

Be Still

Listen and Wait. Be.

Kimberly Brown 6/8 11/14

42

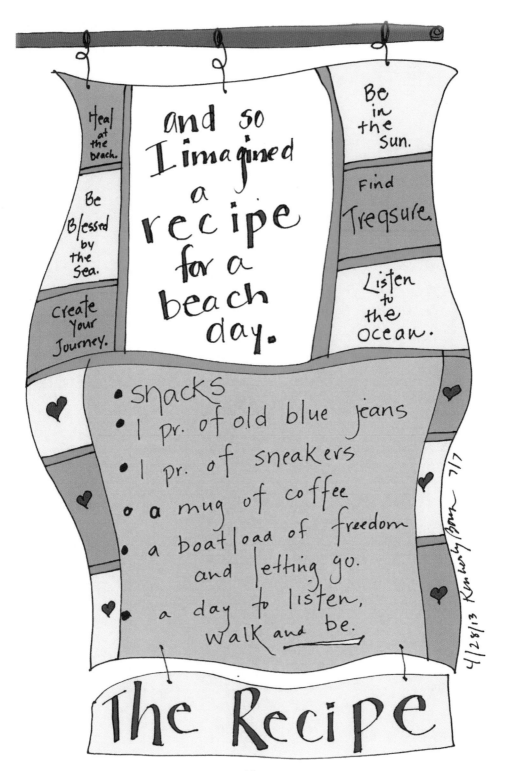

and so
I imagined
a
recipe
for a
beach
day.

Heal at the beach.

Be Blessed by the Sea.

Create Your Journey.

Be in the Sun.

Find Treasure.

Listen to the Ocean.

- snacks
- 1 pr. of old blue jeans
- 1 pr. of sneakers
- a mug of coffee
- a boatload of freedom and letting go.
- a day to listen, walk and be.

The Recipe

4/28/13 Kimberly Brown 7/7

45

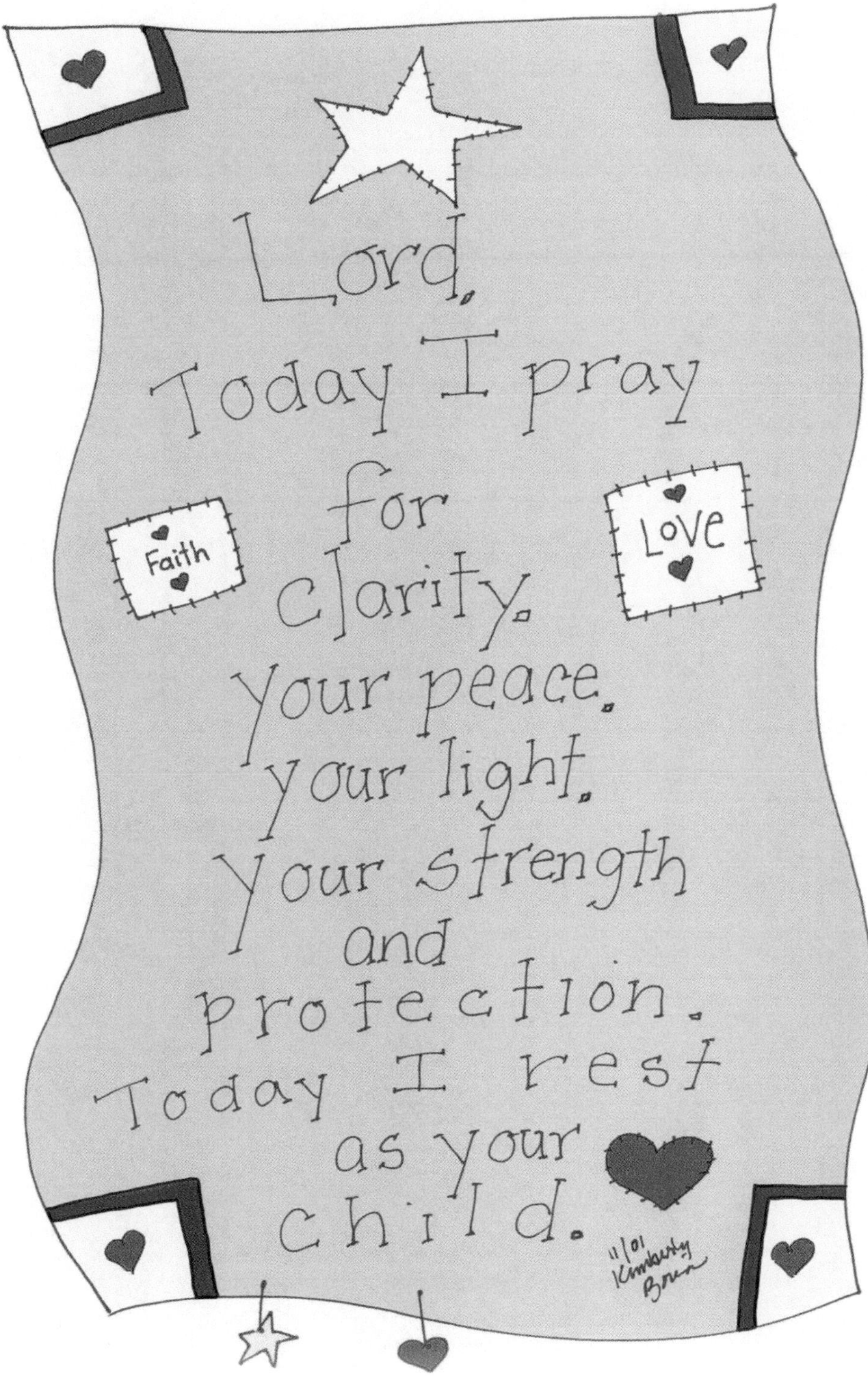

Lord,
Today I pray
for
clarity,
your peace,
your light,
Your strength
and
protection.
Today I rest
as your
child.

11/01
Kimberly
Brun

Faith

Love

Thank You Lord!

Becoming

Blossoming

Gratitude
for
the chances
to laugh
to laugh some more.
to learn anew.
to Be More,
to breathe in
healing
light
to grow, to love
to give, to reach
OUT
to be held by
grace
and love

UR

12/2013 Kimberly Bonn

48

Be Free!

Child,
you are
free,
you are
safe,
you are embraced
by Grace and
the wings of many
magnificent and
loving
Angels.

play

Kimberly Jones 4/8

11/14

49

care

May moments of light, grace, comfort and peace embrace you today.

May warmth, strength and a deep sense of love sustain you.

May you know the gentle presence of mercy and tender whispering grace.

May you believe.

Kimberly Bobic

love

50

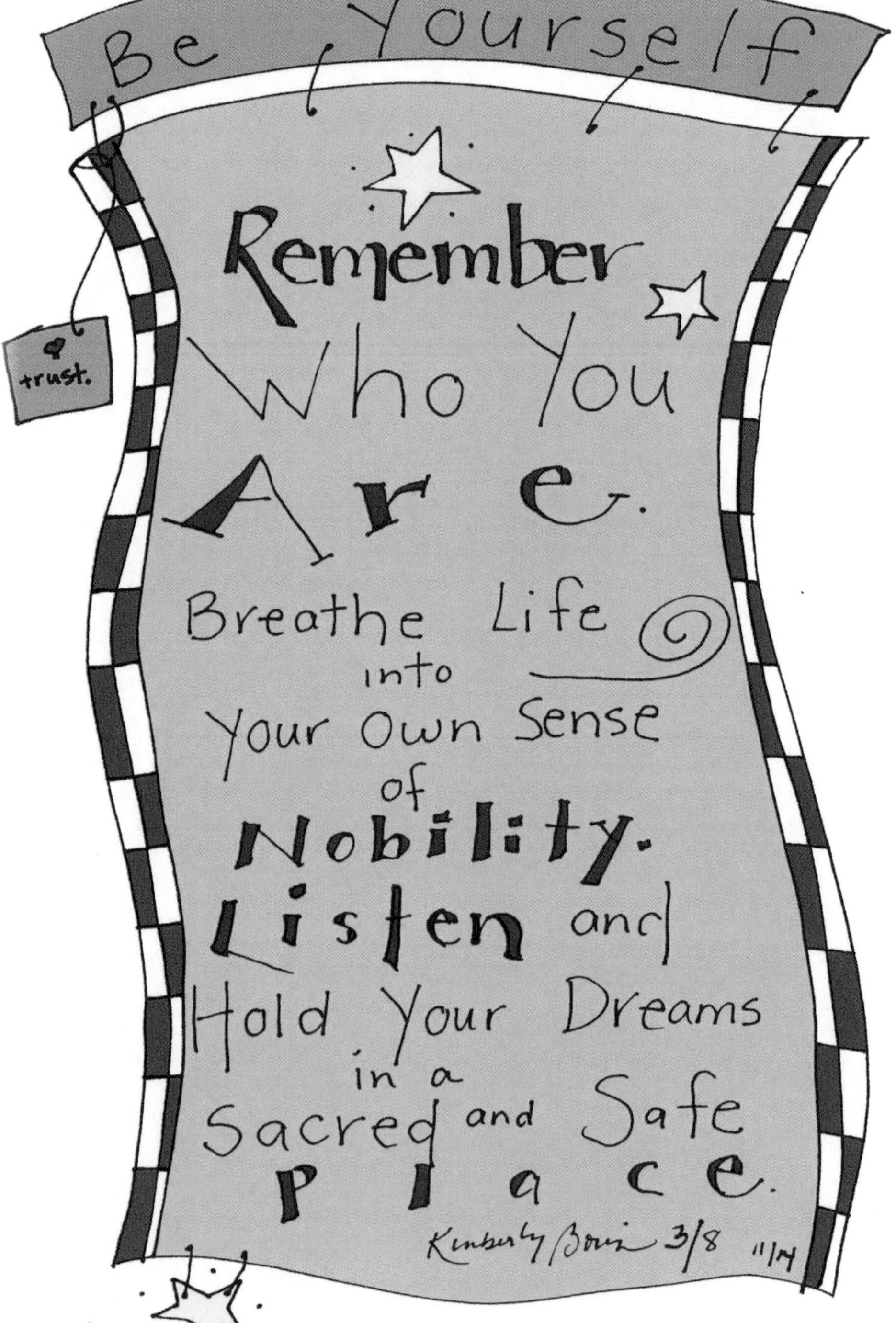

Be Yourself

trust.

Remember
Who You
Are.
Breathe Life
into
Your Own Sense
of
Nobility.
Listen and
Hold Your Dreams
in a
Sacred and Safe
place.

Kimberly Bovis 3/8 11/14

Beautiful
Little
one,
shine
as you are
a b l e.
TRUST
that all of
the light, your
light
is just perfect.
(and enough).

Kimberly Bower 7/8 14/14

Less effort. More God.

54

55

Healing Words

For

The

Journey

Have Faith —

Dream, Believe and Journey

ACT

May you know that your dreams and journey is unfolding in a beautiful way to bring your gift to the world. Believe Friend!

TRUST

10/01 Kimberly

61

faith

sweet!

Blessing

May faith be a bridge and chariot, Carrying you and delivering you safely.

Blessings of faith to you!

10/01 Kimberly

Peace

May peace
wrap around you
like a beautiful
quilt of blessings and
Protection.

love

Wishing You Peace.

you are loved deeply dear friend.

10/01 Kimberly

64

65

Time ♥ Heals

Patience

May patience guide and sustain you in those places of waiting and hope on your journey. ♥

Wishing You Patience.

L O V E !

10/01 Kimberly

67

Grace

May grace present herself to you in all ways — seen and unseen.

Wishing You Grace!

10/01 Kimberly

Strength

May silent strength embrace and uphold you.

Wishing You Strength...

All will be well friend.

10/01 Kimberly

Oh, Tenderness

Perhaps it is time
to celebrate the Warrior of
Tenderness within...

Kimberly
2/21/01

74

75

Balance

Be Still • Listen • Be Loved • Be •

Kimberly
2/21/01

79

Journaling Pages

For You!

Child of Grace,
Take time to rest, to listen, to dream, to be in the
holy knowing that all is well.

Child of Wonder,
Trust that you are blessed and embraced by love,
peace and protection.

Child of Magic and Light,
Shine and sparkle, as only you
know how to do!
(Yes…you are a star!)

Child of the Journey,
Trust that you will be guided each step. Follow
the path of light, playfulness, sweet peace and the
inner smile of joy.
(Yes…you can begin now.)

Child of Play,
You are free to be present to the child within, to partake
in Holy Recess and Playtime.

Child of Love,
You are loved deeply by Angels,
seen and unseen.
(Yes…it is true!)

Child of the Sacred Breath,
Take all of the time that you need to sit, breathe,
and to wait for the
next healing thing to do.
(Breathe beautifully!)

Child of Peace and Vision,
Take time to listen, see, and allow your
future to unfold each miraculous moment.
(It will!)

Child of Stillness and Healing,
Trust that each breath, each step, each small
movement, will bring the grace and healing you
need.

Child of Presence,
Be available to the miracle of life and the holy
presence within and around you. You are blessed.

Child of Gentle Authority and Knowing,
Trust your voice, your story, your gut, and
listening.
Act as you can.

Child of the Creative Gift,
Offer yourself permission to create without
judgment, trusting in your own magnificent
expression.

Child of Compassion
Offer yourself endless compassion complete with
time, gentleness, and quiet.

About the Author

Dr. Kimberly Ann Borin has been working in education since 1989 and has served as an elementary school teacher as well as an elementary and high school counselor. She earned her doctorate in 2005 from Rutgers University in social and philosophical foundations of education. She earned a Master of Education degree in college counseling and student personnel administration from the University of Delaware in 1989 and a Master of Arts degree in educational leadership in 2010 from Centenary College.

She has worked with students in South Africa, Egypt, and Morocco, and as a Fulbright Group Scholar in Swaziland. For her doctoral research, Kimberly gathered children's stories about their favorite moments in nature. She loves to design programs that help children explore and experience mindfulness, relaxation, and resilience in playful and peaceful ways.

Kimberly is also a yoga teacher, certified in the Ananda yoga tradition. She has received level one certification and is registered as an R.Y.T. (Registered Yoga Teacher) at the 200-hour level. She is also trained as a Karma Kids yoga instructor through Karma Kids Yoga in New York City. She is also a certified Laugh Yoga Leader and is trained in Restorative and Therapeutic Yoga. You can find more information on her website, www.theencouragingworks.com.

Whenever she has time (or a snow day from school), Kimberly loves to create art. Her work focuses on words that encourage, uplift, and heal. She creates prints, collages, cards, and yoga mats too! For more information, you can visit www.kimberlyannborin.zenfolio.com.

Kimberly completed a yearlong program in contemplative prayer at the Shalem Institute and is in a second program at the Shalem Institute to lead contemplative prayer groups and retreats. She has been a Reiki healer since 2000. She sees Reiki as a healing energy and a form of contemplative prayer.

She hopes you might check out her first book of memoirs, *Laughter Salad, A Nourishing Mix of Inspiring Stories*, and her second book, *Laughter Salad for Little Ones, A Gentle Mix of Nourishing Letters for Children* and her third book, *Learning and Growing with Laughter Salad*.

40979990R00061

Made in the USA
Charleston, SC
15 April 2015